My Notes

There are only two ways to live your life. One is as though nothing is a miracle. The other is as though everything is a miracle.
—Albert Einstein

My Notes

My Notes

There are only two ways to live your life. One is as though nothing is a miracle. The other is as though everything is a miracle.
—Albert Einstein

My Notes

My Notes

There are only two ways to live your life. One is as though nothing is a miracle. The other is as though everything is a miracle.
—Albert Einstein

My Notes

_____

My Notes

There are only two ways to live your life. One is as though nothing is a miracle. The other is as though everything is a miracle.
—Albert Einstein

My Notes

My Notes

There are only two ways to live your life. One is as though nothing is a miracle. The other is as though everything is a miracle.
—Albert Einstein

My Notes

My Notes

There are only two ways to live your life. One is as though nothing is a miracle. The other is as though everything is a miracle.
—Albert Einstein

My Notes

My Notes

There are only two ways to live your life. One is as though nothing is a miracle. The other is as though everything is a miracle."

—Albert Einstein

My Notes

My Notes

There are only two ways to live your life. One is as though nothing is a miracle. The other is as though everything is a miracle.
—Albert Einstein

My Notes

My Notes

There are only two ways to live your life. One is as though nothing is a miracle. The other is as though everything is a miracle.
—Albert Einstein

My Notes

My Notes

There are only two ways to live your life. One is as though nothing is a miracle. The other is as though everything is a miracle.
—Albert Einstein

My Notes

My Notes

There are only two ways to live your life. One is as though nothing is a miracle. The other is as though everything is a miracle.
—Albert Einstein

My Notes

My Notes

There are only two ways to live your life. One is as though nothing is a miracle. The other is as though everything is a miracle.
—Albert Einstein

My Notes

My Notes

There are only two ways to live your life. One is as though nothing is a miracle. The other is as though everything is a miracle.

—Albert Einstein

My Notes

My Notes

There are only two ways to live your life. One is as though nothing is a miracle. The other is as though everything is a miracle.
—Albert Einstein

My Notes

My Notes

There are only two ways to live your life. One is as though nothing is a miracle. The other is as though everything is a miracle."
—Albert Einstein

My Notes

My Notes

There are only two ways to live your life. One is as though nothing is a miracle. The other is as though everything is a miracle.
—Albert Einstein

My Notes

My Notes

There are only two ways to live your life. One is as though nothing is a miracle. The other is as though everything is a miracle.
— Albert Einstein

My Notes

_____

My Notes

"There are only two ways to live your life. One is as though nothing is a miracle. The other is as though everything is a miracle."
—Albert Einstein

My Notes

_____

My Notes

There are only two ways to live your life. One is as though nothing is a miracle. The other is as though everything is a miracle.
— Albert Einstein

My Notes

My Notes

There are only two ways to live your life. One is as though nothing is a miracle. The other is as though everything is a miracle.

— Albert Einstein

My Notes

My Notes

There are only two ways to live your life. One is as though nothing is a miracle. The other is as though everything is a miracle.
—Albert Einstein

My Notes

My Notes

There are only two ways to live your life. One is as though nothing is a miracle. The other is as though everything is a miracle.
— Albert Einstein

My Notes

My Notes

There are only two ways to live your life. One is as though nothing is a miracle. The other is as though everything is a miracle.
— Albert Einstein

My Notes

My Notes

There are only two ways to live your life. One is as though nothing is a miracle. The other is as though everything is a miracle.
—Albert Einstein

My Notes

My Notes

There are only two ways to live your life. One is as though nothing is a miracle. The other is as though everything is a miracle.
—Albert Einstein

My Notes

My Notes

There are only two ways to live your life. One is as though nothing is a miracle. The other is as though everything is a miracle.
—Albert Einstein

My Notes

My Notes

There are only two ways to live your life. One is as though nothing is a miracle. The other is as though everything is a miracle.
—Albert Einstein

My Notes

My Notes

There are only two ways to live your life. One is as though nothing is a miracle. The other is as though everything is a miracle.
—Albert Einstein

My Notes

My Notes

There are only two ways to live your life. One is as though nothing is a miracle. The other is as though everything is a miracle.

—Albert Einstein

My Notes

My Notes

There are only two ways to live your life. One is as though nothing is a miracle. The other is as though everything is a miracle.

—Albert Einstein

My Notes

My Notes

There are only two ways to live your life. One is as though nothing is a miracle. The other is as though everything is a miracle.
—Albert Einstein

My Notes

My Notes

There are only two ways to live your life. One is as though nothing is a miracle. The other is as though everything is a miracle.
—Albert Einstein

My Notes

My Notes

There are only two ways to live your life. One is as though nothing is a miracle. The other is as though everything is a miracle.
—Albert Einstein

My Notes

My Notes

There are only two ways to live your life. One is as though nothing is a miracle. The other is as though everything is a miracle.
—Albert Einstein

My Notes

_____

My Notes

There are only two ways to live your life. One is as though nothing is a miracle. The other is as though everything is a miracle.
—Albert Einstein

My Notes

My Notes

There are only two ways to live your life. One is as though nothing is a miracle. The other is as though everything is a miracle.
—Albert Einstein

My Notes

My Notes

There are only two ways to live your life. One is as though nothing is a miracle. The other is as though everything is a miracle.
—Albert Einstein

My Notes

My Notes

There are only two ways to live your life. One is as though nothing is a miracle. The other is as though everything is a miracle.
—Albert Einstein

My Notes

_____

My Notes

There are only two ways to live your life. One is as though nothing is a miracle. The other is as though everything is a miracle.
—Albert Einstein

My Notes

My Notes

There are only two ways to live your life. One is as though nothing is a miracle. The other is as though everything is a miracle.
— Albert Einstein

My Notes

My Notes

There are only two ways to live your life. One is as though nothing is a miracle. The other is as though everything is a miracle."
—Albert Einstein

My Notes

My Notes

There are only two ways to live your life. One is as though nothing is a miracle. The other is as though everything is a miracle.
—Albert Einstein

My Notes

My Notes

There are only two ways to live your life. One is as though nothing is a miracle. The other is as though everything is a miracle.
—Albert Einstein

My Notes

My Notes

There are only two ways to live your life. One is as though nothing is a miracle. The other is as though everything is a miracle.
—Albert Einstein

My Notes

My Notes

"There are only two ways to live your life. One is as though nothing is a miracle. The other is as though everything is a miracle."
—Albert Einstein

My Notes

My Notes

There are only two ways to live your life. One is as though nothing is a miracle. The other is as though everything is a miracle.
— Albert Einstein

My Notes

My Notes

"There are only two ways to live your life. One is as though nothing is a miracle. The other is as though everything is a miracle."
—Albert Einstein

My Notes

My Notes

There are only two ways to live your life. One is as though nothing is a miracle. The other is as though everything is a miracle.
— Albert Einstein

My Notes

My Notes

There are only two ways to live your life. One is as though nothing is a miracle. The other is as though everything is a miracle.
—Albert Einstein

My Notes

My Notes

There are only two ways to live your life. One is as though nothing is a miracle. The other is as though everything is a miracle.
— Albert Einstein

My Notes

My Notes

There are only two ways to live your life. One is as though nothing is a miracle. The other is as though everything is a miracle.
— Albert Einstein

My Notes

My Notes

There are only two ways to live your life. One is as though nothing is a miracle. The other is as though everything is a miracle."
—Albert Einstein

My Notes

My Notes

There are only two ways to live your life. One is as though nothing is a miracle. The other is as though everything is a miracle.
—Albert Einstein

My Notes

My Notes

There are only two ways to live your life. One is as though nothing is a miracle. The other is as though everything is a miracle.
—Albert Einstein

My Notes

_____

My Notes

There are only two ways to live your life. One is as though nothing is a miracle. The other is as though everything is a miracle.
—Albert Einstein

My Notes

My Notes

There are only two ways to live your life. One is as though nothing is a miracle. The other is as though everything is a miracle.
—Albert Einstein

My Notes

My Notes

There are only two ways to live your life. One is as though nothing is a miracle. The other is as though everything is a miracle.
—Albert Einstein

My Notes

My Notes

There are only two ways to live your life. One is as though nothing is a miracle. The other is as though everything is a miracle."
—Albert Einstein

My Notes

My Notes

My Notes

There are only two ways to live your life. One is as though nothing is a miracle. The other is as though everything is a miracle.
—Albert Einstein

My Notes

My Notes

There are only two ways to live your life. One is as though nothing is a miracle. The other is as though everything is a miracle.
—Albert Einstein

My Notes

www.ingramcontent.com/pod-product-compliance
Lightning Source LLC
LaVergne TN
LVHW060327080526
838202LV00053B/4435